THE MISADVENTURES OF NICK

THE MISADVENTURES OF NICK

The Memoir of a School Resource Officer
Alameda County Sheriff's Deputy
Floyd W. GILL (RET)

ABOOKS
Alive Book Publishing

Copyright © 2015 by Floyd W. Gill

Additional copies may be ordered from the publisher for educational, business, promotional or premium use. For information, contact ALIVE Book Publishing at: alivebookpublishing.com, or call (925) 837-7303.

Book Design by Alex Johnson
Illustrations by Sharon McClain Gill

ISBN 13
978-1-63132-018-7

ISBN 10
1631320181

Library of Congress Control Number: 2015943381

Library of Congress Cataloging-in-Publication Data
is available upon request.

First Edition

Published in the United States of America
by ALIVE Book Publishing and ALIVE Publishing Group,
imprints of Advanced Publishing LLC
3200 A Danville Blvd., Suite 204, Alamo, California 94507
alivebookpublishing.com

PRINTED IN THE UNITED STATES OF AMERICA

10 9 8 7 6 5 4 3 2 1

Acknowledgments:

I want to thank my wife Sharon and my daughter Kristy for the encouragement to write this book. This book is dedicated to by grand daughters who heard the original stories when they were little girls. Thank you Jordyn, Mackenzie, Ava and Dahlia.

Table of Contents

Foreword

The California Penal Code section 26 states juveniles cannot be arrested if the were under 14 years of age. As a deputy sheriff and school resource officer assigned to juvenile cases I learned that the juvenile justice system is not set up to incarcerate juveniles. The California juvenile justice system would rather teach, counsel and reprimand them then release the juveniles to their parents or legal guardian. Only if the juvenile were a serious violent threat to himself or herself or a violent threat to the community would the juvenile be incarcerated. I was able to use different forms of teaching techniques to teach the juveniles a life lesson and reform their actions. I believe I was successful with many juveniles I had contacted within their schools and many of them were able to change their young lives around and contribute to society. The story of Nick is of one juvenile that refused to accept assistance from his parents, his counselors, his school, juvenile courts or the police.

Chapter One:

The New Position

I had been with the Alameda County Sheriff's Office for about nine years when I got the phone call: "You're going to patrol!" After working jails, courts, and special security details at Oakland Highland Hospital, I was finally being transferred to street patrol. Street patrol was for the elite deputies, and wow! I made it! I was excited and scared at the same time.

I was assigned to an active street beat with ETS (Eden Township Substation). This street beat was everything a rookie like me needed. Dope dealers, dope users and abusers, hookers, a lot of domestic violence victims and domestic violence suspects, petty thieves and young gangbangers. I was a really lucky cop.

What made me even luckier was that I was with two of the best FTOs (field training officers) with ETS patrol division,

Deputy Verlan Blackwell and Deputy Matt Francis. I was with Blackwell for five weeks, and he taught me how to write an excellent police report. I was with my second FTO, Deputy Matt Francis, for five weeks also. Francis was an old-time narcotics officer who really knew his beat. He was very streetwise with a lot of experience and had a great street reputation. All the good guys knew him, all the bad guys knew him, and now I was his trainee. This guy knew his stuff, and now he was training me and teaching me the ropes. Man, was I lucky or what!

I picked up a lot of good tips from FTO Blackwell on how to handle business on my beat. After eight weeks with my FTOs, I was ready to go solo—on my own, ready to hit the streets and to work on my own street reputation.

I did not have a steady beat at first, and had to do my time in the SAP (special assignment and placement) pool. The SAP pool was drawn on to replace any veteran deputy who was on vacation, sick, injured, or had to take time off for any reason. My job in the SAP pool was to take the off-duty deputy's beat. We had eight street beats with two alterative beats, making the SAP pool about ten street beats that covered day shifts, swing shifts, and night shifts.

Being in the SAP pool meant you could work day shift for a week, night shift the next week, and swing shift another week. It was great for a rookie like me because it meant I worked all the beats. I thought that would make me the best street deputy in the division. I was hoping to make my mark wherever they placed me.

While in the SAP pool I made a few good busts that made the news. I guess I was in the right place at the right time. I made my FTO proud, and it appeared I was on the right track and going somewhere fast.

Then one day I noticed that my name was not on the SAP pool schedule. "What's going on?" I asked the desk sergeant.

"Just go home. You'll get a call about your beat assignment.

Don't worry, it's just an oversight by the watch lieutenant."

When I made it home I noticed the red light blinking on my telephone answering machine. On the playback it was my lieutenant. "This is Lieutenant Hogue. You've been selected for a new position. This position is the sheriff's, baby, so listen up! You are the new school resource officer assigned to the Castro Valley School District. Report to the Crime Prevention sergeant's office on Monday morning and he will fill you in on your assignment. Congratulations and don't screw it up!"

"What!!" I wondered. "What did I do wrong?! I made some great busts! I'm a good beat deputy! Am I on the crap list? What is a school resource officer? Why make me a kiddie cop? How do I get out of this detail? What the hell is going on with this new job!"

On Monday I reported to Sergeant Elkridge in the Crime Prevention Division and my new job. My uniform was pressed and my boots were spit-shined. I'm the new SRO, the cop assigned to the high school.

I was sure all the deputies were going to razz me. Cops are ruthless when it comes to razzing. And I got razzed well at morning patrol muster; then as I walked down the hall to see the Crime Prevention sergeant all I could hear was "Look at the new kindergarten cop! Ha, ha, ha," and "Hey, Gill, make sure you check all the kids for their hall passes. Ha, ha, ha."

I finally made it down that long hallway and stood in the doorway to the Crime Prevention sergeant's office, not knowing what to do. Do I go in?

My new sergeant is on the phone. He motions for me to come in and take a seat near his desk. I'm sitting there waiting for him to finish his phone conversation.

In my mind I'm still wondering, What am I doing here? I'm a street cop now, not a juvenile cop. What am I supposed to do at the high school? This is the Sheriff's program, so how can I get out of this detail and stay in the Patrol Division? Maybe this program won't last long and I can return to real crooks and real crime. I want to make the streets safe from criminals! Get off the phone, Sergeant, so I can get going and get off duty.

Finally the sergeant hung up the phone and was looking at me. He asked me, "So what do you know about the SRO program?"

My answer was "Nothing. I thought you were going to tell me what to do."

The sergeant asked, "Then why did they pick you to be the SRO?"

My answer was "I don't know, I though you knew."

"Well, I guess that makes the two of us that don't know, since I don't know what this program is all about," said the sergeant. "You are going to have to learn on the fly."

So the sergeant told me to drive to the high school and ask for the principal, who was waiting for me in her office. Maybe she can tell you what they want you to do for them at the high school. After this speech and so-called pep rally, the sergeant picked up the telephone and made another call.

I stood there for a few seconds and I thought, "Hey, this is the Sheriff's, baby, so don't screw up." I went out to my patrol car and prepared for my day.

I finally left the patrol station and I drove toward the high school. It didn't take long and suddenly there I was at my new beat. The high school! What am I going to do? What am I doing here? How the hell do I get back to the mean streets? I'm a crime fighter!!

I drove around the high school three times, wondering what to do. I drove around the campus, not knowing my mission. I drove through the student parking lot and noticed some graffiti on a school maintenance building, and I wondered, What is that all about?

As I continued to drive through the student parking lot, I noticed two girls standing near a car. I thought they were leaving campus, so I came to a slow stop to just watch them. They had a short conversation about something and then they quickly walked back toward the school campus. I guess they decided not to cut school that morning. Good work.

Well, I figured I needed to go to the principal's office and report in. I decided to make one more trip around the campus before I finally stopped in front of the school.

I noticed two adult males sitting in a parked car in front of the school. I know dope dealers when I see them, and these dope dealers looked when I saw them. I gave them the look of disapproval, and then pulled over to the curb and just observed them. I wanted to make them nervous. I noticed they had a brief conversation and quickly started up their car and drove off. I watched them drive off, and I followed them in my patrol car with the disapproval look. It looked like they decided not to hang around the high school today. Another good job!!

I couldn't put it off much longer. The principal and assistant principals are waiting for me. I pulled over to the curb in front of the school and got out of my patrol car. I felt like a kid again— I couldn't believe I had to go to the principal's office!

I followed the signs on the hallway to the principal's office and walked over to the secretary's desk. The secretary said, "Welcome. We've been waiting for you. I'm Mrs. Parker, the principal's secretary."

"Thanks, who is the principal?" I asked.

"That will be Mrs. Tina Karp, and they are all waiting for you in her office." I walked into her office and they were all there waiting. Mrs. Karp and assistant principals Mr. Jerry Green, Mrs. Dian Pico, and Mrs. Leslie Rothwell.

They invited me over to a large conference table and began to ask me questions. "So, what do you know about the SRO program?"

"Nothing," I answered.

"Why did they pick you?"

"I don't know," I answered.

"Do you like kids?" they asked.

"Well, I can deal with kids because I'm familiar with young people. I was a former sergeant in the Marine Corps with a lot of young troops."

They looked at me with questions still in their heads. Then the principal asked, "What can you do to help us?"

My answer was "I can do anything you need for assistance! I don't know what problems you have now, so what do you need help with and what do you want?"

The principal said, "We want you to make our campus safe."

And my reply was, "Well, I drove around the campus a little before coming in. Here is what I saw and what I don' like. I don't like seeing students out of class and standing in the student parking lot. I don't like seeing graffiti on school buildings, and I don't like seeing dope dealers hanging around in front of your school campus."I finished by saying, "I'm the kind of guy who takes care of my beat, so If I'm going to stay I plan on taking action to clean up my beat."

All four school administrators began to smile as one, giving me a loud "Yeah, we have been waiting for you! Welcome!"

Principal Karp made a special announcement over the school PA system. She informed all the teachers and students that the new SRO was on campus and that my name was Officer Gill. She invited all the staff and students to approach me when seen on campus and all students and staff to welcome me to their school.

Assistant Principal Jerry Green asked me to join him in the center courtyard to meet some of the kids. It was time for snack break and passing period, and it was his turn to supervise students during the break. We both stood in the center of the campus courtyard, and before I knew it there were thousands of students all surrounding us.

They would walk up and ask, "What are you doing here?"

and "You should be in Oakland and not here, we don't need you here!"

I calmly said, "Consider me like a fire hydrant: you don't use a fire hydrant until there is a fire. I'm here in case there is a fire."

Mr. Green said to me, "Don't pay any attention to them, we need you on campus." The school bell rang and they all went back to class.

I walked around the inner area of the school to become familiar with the campus. I walked up and down the halls.

After what seemed to be a long time, I noticed the school lunch period was approaching. I returned to my patrol car to watch students leaving campus for lunch.I positioned by patrol car near the student parking lot exit so that all drivers would see my blue and gold patrol car with the blue and red emergency overhead lights. I'm ready for my first speeder.

The school bell rang and students began to slowly drive off campus and leave for lunch. No action and no tickets. Now what to do? I know! I'll drive through the student parking lot. Maybe I'll catch someone writing graffiti on the maintenance building.

As I drove through the student parking lot I noticed a group of students running toward the other end of the parking lot. Where were they going? Now I see a problem. A student fight. Now I have action—and on my first day.

When I drew closer to the large crowd, I noticed one student was bleeding from a head wound and could see another student with a baseball bat in his hand. I bet that was my suspect and the student with the head injury was my victim. That's called a clue in law enforcement.

I put out an emergency dispatch call for an ambulance and approached the student with the baseball bat to take him into custody. I grabbed him and took the bat away from his grip.

Students were yelling, "They are all gang members from Hayward!" and they pointed to two other students standing near a car with its doors open.I ordered them to freeze and was able to take them into custody as well. The emergency sirens heard in the background responding to my location helped, so they knew running was no use. Now I had three nonstudents in custody for assault with a deadly weapon.

Backup units were arriving, and the students looked relieved even though they were still excited about seeing a fight on their campus. Assistant Principal Green and campus supervisors arrived to supervise students and to inform the principal about the fight on campus. I gave him a brief statement about being in the right area at the right time.

Now I had something to do. I had three juveniles in custody for a felony assault and I was an eyewitness to the entire incident. What a good first day! The kindergarten cop had three felony arrests at a school.

When I returned to the patrol station, there were no more smart remarks about the SRO not having anything to do but check hall passes.

The next day, all the school staff had good remarks to say about the fight on campus. I heard a lot of thank-yous from staff and parents. Even some of the same kids who wanted me to go to Oakland were happy to see me on campus. I guess they all have a new respect for fire hydrants!

Chapter 2

Hello, Bobby,
and Good–Bye Old Friend

My first day as the new SRO went well, with three nonstudents in custody and the smart-mouth kids thinking again about why I was there. Things were starting to come together.

That's when I noticed him. A special-education student was following me around. He was close behind me, asking me my name. I stopped and told him that I was the SRO and he could call me Officer Gill. He told me his name was Bobby.

Bobby told me he had to go to class, and he asked me to escort him there. Bobby wanted all his classmates to see us together. I told him to lead the way, and I met his special education teacher, Mrs. Reed.

I learned Bobby has diagnosed with Asperger's Syndrome,

and he required a lot of attention for his special needs. I was informed that Bobby tends to latch on to someone in uniform.

Bobby became my new backup; I noticed he was always there when I arrived on campus. Bobby would sit on the curb in front of the school and just wait for me to arrive for work. He refused to go to class until I arrived. Whenever I passed by his classroom, Bobby would leave and follow me around.

I recall on one occasion having to direct traffic after a minor auto accident near the student parking lot, and noticing Bobby standing directly behind me imitating my hand and arm gestures to direct traffic.

Soon other special-education students in Bobby's class wanted to join him and wait for my arrival. Bobby introduced me to his best friend, Jamal. Jamal was a kid who had a lot of respect for men in uniform. Bobby and Jamal wanted to follow me everywhere on campus.

I was responsible for all the elementary schools as well as the high school. I was assigned to two middle schools, one continuation high school, and eight elementary schools. My schedule was very hectic at times, but I could always count on Bobby to look for me somewhere on campus.

One morning as I parked my patrol car, Bobby ran up to me to show me that he had a badge. His neighbor had given him a toy metal badge that was the same shape as my badge. Bobby wanted me to inscribe my badge number into his badge. He was very excited about the idea of having the same badge number as mine. The student services clerk had an electric etching machine, and I was able to print my badge number on Bobby's toy badge. Bobby went to class happy that day. He even had a wallet that he secured the badge in, so he could pretend to be an undercover officer. What a happy kid now.

One day I noticed a small group of kids watching Bobby and Jamal laughing with me. I overheard one student say, "Look at the retards!" I decided to call that student over to have a private conversation. I told that student that Bobby and Jamal were special-education students and that they were my friends. I told that student that if Bobby and Jamal were having a bad day at school because of him or his friends, I would make sure that he and all his friends had a bad day at school as well. He left with a good understanding that Bobby and Jamal were not to be harassed.

Later that week was high school homecoming. The entire school was set for a good time. The school made special arrangements for fireworks at halftime, and a group of skydivers were going to land on the football field. It was going to be a special event to show off school pride.

I worked the football game, and my partners Bobby and Jamal were there to help. As the halftime fireworks began and the skydivers were slowly descending on the football field's fifty-yard line, Jamal had something to tell me. He had seen a student with a handgun in his waistband.

I asked Jamal where the student with the handgun was, and he pointed to the grandstand bleachers. Jamal took me over to the foot of the bleachers, and he pointed to a student he identified as "Tommy," sitting near the top of the grandstands. As Jamal was pointing to the student, that student saw Jamal was identifying him. He immediately got up and started trying to make an escape. He was trying to make it through the crowd to the opposite end of the bleachers. Meanwhile, everyone else was watching the skydivers land in the center of the football field. With all the cheers, no one paid attention to Jamal or me.

I decided to walk quickly around the bleachers to stop the student at the other end. I waited in the dark to catch my suspect. It worked because as I made it to the other end of the bleachers he had come down to flat land and was approaching me. I grabbed him from behind and told him he was under arrest. He was really surprised.

I asked him if he had a gun on him and he said, "It's my father's gun!" and "I'm not supposed to have it!"

I placed handcuffs on the student and asked him his name. "Tommy" was his reply. I reached into his waistband area and pulled out a semiautomatic handgun. I escorted Tommy to my patrol car. Sixteen-year-old Tommy pleaded with me not to tell his father that he took his handgun. As I placed Tommy in the backseat of the patrol car and secured the handgun in the patrol car's trunk, I noticed a large fight breaking out in the parking lot. I called for backup. Things were getting out of control.

Once Tommy was secured in the locked patrol car, I ran over to break up the fight. I noticed a student was bleeding profusely around the neck and hands. I immediately called for an ambulance for him. Then I noticed a group of students running down the street trying to escape. I chased after one who allegedly slashed the victim with a box cutter. I saw him jump over a fence and was able to catch him hiding in a backyard. I placed handcuffs on him and escorted him off the property.

His spontaneous statement to me was, "They made me do it." I escorted my suspect back onto campus and placed him in the backseat with Tommy. What a night! Two felony arrests made in less than half an hour.

Backup arrived and began helping with the crowd. The student with the large slash was taken to the hospital, and I made arrangements to take his statement once I had secured my two felony arrestees. It was going to be a long night.

To make it exciting, I drove to the police station to start my paperwork. Paperwork is always exciting. I was about a mile away from the high school when all of a sudden I noticed a senior citizen stepping out into the middle of the street to flag my patrol car down. I stopped to ask what was wrong.

The senior citizen said, "That's my house, but that is not my truck in the driveway." As he told me his story he pointed to a house with a pickup truck backed up in the driveway. I put out the call to emergency dispatch that a possible home burglary was in progress, and then noticed that the truck had a driver sitting behind the wheel watching us.

I then observed a male adult placing tools in the back of the pickup truck. At the same time he too noticed we were watching them. I had to act fast, so I quickly exited my patrol car and drew my service weapon.

I ordered the man at the back of the truck to the ground and the driver out of the truck. The driver was a woman, and she took her time but did as she was ordered to do. I held the two suspects at gunpoint until backup arrived. The two suspects were handcuffed and the owner of the house interviewed.

The homeowner stated that he came home and noticed the pickup truck backed into his driveway. He was on his way to a neighbor to call 911 when he spotted my patrol car. He stated that he did not know the man or the woman and that he wanted to place them under citizen's arrest. The two burglars were both on parole. Who would have thought?

What a night! Four felony arrests in less than an hour and a half. And Jamal had done a great job as my backup. What do you think of the kiddie cop now?

Then tragedy happened. It was December 11, 1998, when an Alameda County Deputy Sheriff assigned to the City of Dublin was murdered. Deputy John Paul Monego was shot and killed as he entered the Outback Steakhouse restaurant answering a 911 call. John was shot as he walked through the front door of the restaurant. He did not know it at the time, but three suspects had decided to do a take-over robbery, and they had been able to take the first responding deputy hostage and disarm her.

This murdered deputy was a friend of mine. His locker was next to mine in the police locker room. I saw John daily, and joked with him often. John worked the night shift and I worked the day shift, but we shared the same patrol car. Everyone in my department was in shock.

I was off duty the day John was murdered, and I volunteered to work his shift that night. When my shift ended, the dispatcher informed me that I had at least fifty messages waiting for me. The caller was a juvenile, and he had called all night wanting to speak with me only. It was Bobby.

Bobby was concerned that I would get hurt like my friend John, and he wanted me to pick him up so that he could watch over me as I patrolled the city. Bobby did not understand what was happening. He begged me to pick him up because he was my backup. I finally convinced Bobby that I was all right and that I would see him at school.

John's funeral was five days later, and the entire city was in mourning. Bobby stood on the sidewalk like all the other citizens to show respect to my friend John. It was a sad day in my career, but Bobby was there to make it better. Thank you, Bobby. Thank you, Jamal.

R.I.P John Monego

Chapter 3

Meeting Nick

That's when I got the call: I had to go to one of the elementary schools to check on the welfare of a ten-year-old boy. I checked in with Principal Jack Baker, and he gave me a brief idea about why he called and what his concerns were.

The principal informed me that a ten-year-old named Nick was left on his own to get dressed for school, and he suspected that Nick's mother was leaving him alone every night. I was told the mother was hard to make contact with by telephone and that she might have a night job. The principal said there were no adults living in the apartment who were able to help Nick, and he also said the kids at school were telling him that Nick was not going to have a Christmas.

I drove over to the listed address and left a business card for Laura, Nick's mother, to call me regarding her son. I spoke with neighbors and very little was known about the family. I returned to the school and took Nick into protective custody.

First we went through a drive-through restaurant to get Nick something to eat. This was a big deal for Nick, as he was very hungry. As he ate he really opened up about his mother, Laura.

I learned that his father had left many years prior and that he had never met the man. I learned that he had a grandmother, but she was sick and lived out of state. Then I learned that his mother left home every night to go out and that she wore a uniform like a waitress.

As I sat with the Nick at the police station, an unknown woman called dispatch to report a juvenile missing from the school where I had collected Nick. I instructed dispatch to have the woman report to the station to collect Nick and give additional information on Laura's status.

Well, the woman arrived at the station and I learned that she was a friend of Laura and that she had been sent to the school to pickup Nick but had run late. Now I had an adult who could make the situation clearer. Where was Laura, and what was going on?

I learned that Laura had a day job as well as a night job as a waitress and that she was having a tough time trying to make ends meet. I was able to contact Laura on the telephone and explained that other arrangements needed to be made regarding Nick.

Laura agreed to meet with me at her apartment so that I could inspect the premises. In the meantime, Nick had met the station secretary, Barbra; Barbra had taken a liking to Nick and wanted to help him and his mother. Barbra wanted to go to the apartment with Nick and me.

When Barbra walked into the apartment with me, we could both see that there were no Christmas decorations in the apartment. Little Nick was not going to have a Christmas; so Barbra immediately went into action. She met with another station secretary, named Liz, and the two women took Nick and went to the grocery store to buy Nick food and cleaning supplies.

They returned to the apartment with fresh milk, cereal, cans of soup, chili, hot dogs, cheese, fresh hamburger meat, and a turkey with all the fixings for Christmas dinner. Nick had a big smile on his face because he had his favorite chocolate chip cookies and chocolate ice cream for dessert.

It was weird to see uniformed deputies washing dishes and vacuuming the carpet. We all began to decorate and clean the apartment to help Barbra and Liz.

One of the beat officers, named Bob, knew a man who ran a Christmas tree lot on his beat, and he convinced the owner to donate a Christmas tree for Nick. He then went home to collect tree lights to decorate the tree. Now I had Barbra, Liz, and Bob at Nick's apartment.

Beat officer Dave heard about what was going on, and he drove to the toy store on his beat and bought several toys for Nick. Not wanting to be left out, other beat officers were in the toy store buying toys, books, and puzzles as well.

I could not believe it, but it started to look as if the entire police station was coming in and out of Nick's apartment, repairing the place and making it look like Christmas.

Nick's mother, Laura, soon arrived, and she immediately began to cry when she saw the Christmas tree in her living room. She told us she had been working hard to give Nick a Christmas. It was good to see Nick and Laura hugging and crying in their apartment. Then Barbra and Liz began to flood the room with tears, and even those hardened street cops were choking back tears. This is what I had always wanted to do: help people who need help

I gave Laura the name and number of Social Services and informed her that I would follow up with the agency and arrange for Nick to receive lunch at school when Christmas break ended.

I met with the principal, Jack, before school closed for Christmas break and informed him that I had made contact with Laura and that she was working hard to keep Nick out of the courts.

Merry Christmas, Nick! Merry Christmas, Barbra and Liz! Merry Christmas, ETS patrol!

Chapter 4

Left Home Alone
The Wake Up Call

I had not seen Nick in a year or so and assumed he was doing well when I had to deal with another troubled youth named Raymond. A junior at Castro Valley High School at the time, Raymond was a real pain for school administrators. The deputies working the Castro Valley patrol were very familiar with him. Raymond liked to hang around with three other troubled young men, each one trying to outdo the other at stupid pranks and activities.

One day, I was near the school when Raymond and his friends were cutting school. When they saw my patrol car they ran and tried to hide behind some bushes. A dog in a nearby fenced yard began barking and alerted me to their presence.

When I caught Raymond and his friends, they reacted with what could best be described as a "serious attitude." They claimed to know their rights and loudly protested my interference in their "leisure activities." They apparently had to learn the hard way that they did not have the right to cut school.

I drove the four boys back to school and the school secretary said, "Oh no, not again, can't you four stay out of trouble?" I said, "I guess they are in the vice principal's office all the time." She responded saying, "Oh yes, they are all frequent flyers." As I waited for the vice principal, the boys laughed, thinking their troubles were just a big joke.

Vice-principal Green came out and asked, "What did they do today?" I briefed him on their cutting school and running from me when that spotted my patrol car. Mr. Green asked me to wait for one of Raymond's parents because he thought I might be interested in seeing Raymond's interaction with them. About ten minutes later Raymond's mother, Evelyn, arrived. Upon seeing his mother, Raymond lost control, and cursed at her. I stood at the office door because he tried to leave. Raymond and I stood toe-to-toe, eye-to- eye at the office door and I calmly told him to sit down and calm down. I believe that was the first time any adult ever stood up to Raymond.

Raymond was suspended for cutting school and he and his mother left campus. After they left the office, I learned from assistant principal Green that Raymond and his friends were responsible for throwing field mice in classrooms causing total chaos in classrooms for students and the teacher. On another occasion they threw a live garter snake into the girl's locker room during PE changing time. They were also responsible for buying live crickets and grasshoppers from a local pet store and setting the insects loose in the school cafeteria. That caused total pandemonium during the lunch period. Students were afraid of the four boys because they were afraid of retaliation. I was told that I would see a lot more of these four troublemakers in the future.

Shortly thereafter, a teacher called to say that Raymond was in a heated argument with his mother in the campus parking lot. I walked out to assist Evelyn but as I approached her Raymond walked off campus in an angry tirade. I saw him curse his mother as he walked away. He then gave me "the finger" as he turned and walked away.

Evelyn said, "Raymond is my only child. He is always angry with me and his dad and we don't know what to do." She began to cry and said, "I'm losing my son." I gave her the phone number to a counseling service and I suggested the family attend counseling together.

Later that night the midnight shift caught Raymond and his three friends drinking beer behind the Castro Valley bowling alley. The deputies took the boys home after reprimanding them again for their misbehavior. When the midnight deputies made contact with Raymond's parents, Evelyn and Bruce, the deputies almost recommended that Raymond go to a psychiatric ward for observation because they thought Raymond he might be suicidal. He was a very angry kid.

The next day Raymond and his friends continued to terrorize the community. They would often sneak out at night, vandalizing the neighborhood. I encountered the four boys on several occasions, and sadly, each experience was negative. I called them the "my rebels without a clue." Because of their antics it was a long summer in Castro Valley that year.

In 1997, Raymond was a senior at Castro Valley High School. His class would graduate in mid June of 1998. Raymond would celebrate his 18th birthday in late May, three weeks before graduation.

His parents often told him that things would change for him on his 18th birthday. Raymond would curse them and say, "I can't wait to turn 18 and get away from you two a*** holes!"

The big day came. It was Raymond's birthday and he got up to go to school—not to go to class, but only to see his friends. He walked into the kitchen where his parents were eating breakfast and once again began cursing. He put some bacon between a couple slices of bread and told his parents he was on his way to school. His mother said, "Happy Birthday son," to which Raymond growled, "Just leave me alone you fat bi***h—it's my birthday." Raymond's father, Bruce, said, "When you get home from school, we have a surprise for you." Raymond responded saying, "You better have bought me a car for my birthday, you a** hole."

Raymond met with his three friends and they decided to go to one of their houses and drink beer and smoke pot. They wanted to do anything but go to school because, after all, it was Raymond's birthday!

Raymond made it back home around 7:00 pm. When he unlocked the front door the surprise was there—the house was empty. His parents moved away when he should have been in school. Raymond's parents took all their personal belongings, all their furniture and left without a hint as to where they were going. The house was a rental so they had to leave the refrigerator and the stove but the only thing not taken was Raymond's bedroom furniture.

He found a note on the kitchen counter that read, "Happy Birthday Son...Surprise!" Raymond was in shock that his parents would move without giving him a hint of their new location. I was working overtime that evening when the emergency dispatcher gave me that all too familiar address of Raymond's house. The dispatcher said, "Contact a juvenile named Raymond that wanted to speak only to you about his parents." I was expecting the worst. Deputy Suchon heard the broadcast for service and he responded as my cover deputy in case there was a problem.

I knocked on the front door and I heard Raymond say, "Come in." When I walked into Raymond's house I was surprised. He walked towards me and said, "They moved away officer Gill. Today is my birthday and they just moved and left me."

Deputy Suchon arrived a short time later and joined us in the living room. Suchon's response was, "Looks like they moved away." I told Suchon, "Today is Raymond's 18th birthday so what do you recommend as a birthday gift?" Suchon responded, "Furniture would be a nice gift to start." Raymond asked me, "Officer Gill, what should I do?"

As an old school Marine Corp platoon sergeant, I did not sugar coat my opinion when I felt things had to be said. I said to Raymond, "What do you think Raymond? You have not been a good son to your parents for a long time. I overheard you on numerous occasions curse your parents and you have done a lot of things to make their lives a living hell. Eighteen years ago today your mother gave you life and your words have cut her heart like a knife. Your dad and I gave her a lot of tissues to dry her tears because of your sharp tongue. Their decision to move away was a hard one and your mother may be still crying for leaving you behind. They were sick of YOUR disrespect and finally just moved away. You must own up to what you have done to make them move. Wake up Raymond and welcome to the adult world."

Raymond broke down and began to cry. "What am I going to do now?" he asked. I said, "Adults make a plan, so let's sit down and make a plan." Raymond said the house was a rental and the landlord lived next door. I knocked on the landlord's door and asked about his former tenants, Raymond's parents. The landlord, Mr. Stevens, said that they paid the rent for the month of May and did not leave any information as to their new address. Mr. Stevens then told Raymond that he had until the end of the month to move out because he had a new couple planning on moving into the house in July.

Raymond had a lost look on his face. He was still in shock. To make things complicated, his three friends (the three stooges) were waiting outside to visit. They went into the house and said, "Wow, that's really f***ed up. They can't like just leave because, that's like child abuse or something." I told them, "Raymond is no longer a juvenile. Today is his 18th birthday and he is now an adult." They were in shock like Raymond. I told Raymond, "Send your friends home because you are no longer a slap in the wrist juvenile. If you do something stupid today you go to Santa Rita jail with all the other adults".

I suggested we come up with a plan over pizza. I took Raymond to a pizza parlor to celebrate his birthday and we came up with a plan. The plan included meeting with him the next day to work on cleaning up his house and maybe getting his parents cleaning deposit back.

I dropped him off at home after pizza and I told Raymond to, "Stay at home tonight because if you get into trouble from now on you will go to adult jail and there will be no one around to bail you out, leaving you with a new jail house cell mate that will be happy to see a new face in his cell." Raymond agreed and he slowly walked into his empty house.

The next day I was off duty and returned to Raymond's house to take him around to look for a job. I told him fast food restaurants were probable hiring but it was only a temporary fix. Then I drove him to a strip mall that was the offices for all the military recruiters.

We stood in the parking lot and read large letters advertising Army, Navy, Air Force and Marine Corps. Raymond asked me, "What do you think?" Like before, I gave my opinion without sugar coating it.

I told him that I graduated from high school in 1969 and I joined the Marine Corps after graduation. I also added that it was the right decision for me. I server two tours of duty in Viet Nam and it was the still the right decision for me. I told him about half the deputies on my department had served in the military and it was the right decision for them as well.

I said, "There is good as well as bad in joining the military." We made a mental list of both good and bad. I told Raymond here are the good, in my opinion. You will get free clothing (uniforms), free housing (barracks), free food three times a day, free medical and dental, if your unit has to travel overseas you get to visit new lands and see the world, you earn college credit under the GI education bill which is a good idea, because I used my GI education bill to earn a degree in criminal justice and without fail, every two weeks you get a government paycheck. Just open a savings account so that you will have money when you discharge from the military.

The bad: You will get a lot of exercise, they will work you long and hard and they will be in your face if they think you are not motivated in doing your job. They will demand that you and your new friends keep your barracks clean as well as keeping your body clean. You will have to stop drinking and smoking weed because they have a code that is strictly enforced through the Uniform Code of Military Justice. If you violate the code they will throw you in the stockade and they will sentence you to hard labor until you can demonstrate you will follow the military code. Without the code your life and everyone else's life is in danger.

They will test you to find a job that you can perform well and they will send you to many schools to help you do a good job, and they will demand that you do your job well every day. And finally, if the military is drawn into a war you will have to go with your unit and your new friends to honor your commitment.

The United States is not at war now but there are people out there that hate America and they hate what we stand for. They hate our freedom and they hate our life style. If our country comes under attack the military will be activated and called upon to defend our nation. A lot of brave young men and women will put their lives in harm's way to defend or great nation.

If we went to war I would be happy to grab a rifle and put on by boots and walk into combat, but they won't call me because I'm considered too old—but they will call you. Are you willing to join those brave young men and women?"

I ended saying, "It's a big decision so take your time." We waited for about five minutes and he said, "My dad was in the army. Let's go in and see the army recruiter." I walked onto the office with him and introduced Raymond to the army recruit sergeant. The sergeant stood up and said, "Welcome Raymond," extending his hand. I told Raymond that I would wait for him outside and left the office. It was a good thing that I had a magazine in my truck because Raymond was with the recruiter for about two hours.

When Raymond left the recruiter's office I saw that he had a few brochures in his hands. "Well?" I asked, and Raymond said, "I joined the army." "When do you ship out?" I again asked. He told me he had to report to Fort Hood Texas at the end of June. "Well," I said, "we should come up with a plan because you will be leaving soon." I suggested that he ask his landlord, Mr. Stevens, who happen to be a WWII army veteran, if he could store his furniture in his half empty garage until he completed boot camp and basic training. I said, "Stand in front of him, look him in the eye, and give his hand a firm hand shake—then tell him your new plan." I also suggested Raymond mow the front lawn to show his landlord that he should take a chance and grant him that favor.

I dropped Raymond off at his house so he could continue cleaning, then I drove to my house to get my lawn mower. I unloaded the lawn mower into my pick-up truck and Raymond began mowing the front lawn. When he finished mowing, I loaded the lawn mower back into my pick-up truck as I watched Raymond walk over to his landlord and shake his hand.

Raymond walked over to me and said, "Mr. Stevens will store by stuff until I finish basic training." A couple of minutes later we saw his friends walking down the street towards his house. I said, "Don't let those three stooges blow your plans now because they don't have anything to lose. You're an adult now and you will be the big loser if you land in jail with some angry ex-con looking for a new roommate. That ex-con would be willing to sell you to anyone for a couple packs of cigarettes after abusing you." Raymond said, "I'm done with them and I'll send them away."

Three weeks later it was graduation day. Raymond was going to walk across the stage and get his high school diploma. I believe every teacher and school staff member was happy to finally see Raymond and his friends leave. Raymond kept looking for his parents and he was hoping that they would attend his graduation, but they were not there. I attended the graduation, however—in fact, I was always there for graduation because I was the district's school resource officer. Raymond saw me and was happy to finally graduate, but at the same time he was sad because his parents were not there to see him in his finest hour.

At the end of June, I drove Raymond to the military recruiter office. I shook his hands and said goodbye. Raymond joined the other recruits and was off to Fort Hood Texas.

Five or six months later, Raymond was back in Castro Valley to claim his bedroom furniture. Raymond stopped by his old high school to visit his teachers and to show off his uniform. Everyone was surprised to see the "new" Raymond. He stood straight and tall and proud in his clean, pressed uniform with spit-shined boots. We could not believe our eyes. What a change; from the old "Punk Kid Raymond," to the new, "Army-proud Raymond." He told me that he was on his way to Fort Bragg, North Carolina to join the 82nd airborne. Joking, I said, "Why would you want to jump out of a perfectly good airplane?" Raymond joked back, "Because it is something to do, I guess."

I called Deputy Suchon, who had served in the Marine Corps like me, and invited him to the high school to see the new Raymond. We were all blown away.

Then came September 11, 2001. In October, the army launched Operation Enduring Freedom with the 82nd airborne division spearheading the fight in Afghanistan. Raymond was assigned with that army division. Before leaving for Afghanistan, he called me at the police station and asked for some advice. Having seen combat in Vietnam, I had some experience, so I told him to, "Just find a good sergeant and listen to him. The sergeant is the army, not the officers. The officers think they are in charge but the sergeants really run the army. If you listen to your sergeant you will walk out of combat alive with your sergeant." Raymond said, "That sounds like a good advice and I'll do just that".

Later, in 2003, the army launched Operation Iraqi Freedom and the 82nd airborne division was involved in that campaign. I did not hear from Raymond at the end of each operation and hoped he was doing well. Finally, in the winter of 2008, I received a telephone call at the police station from Raymond. He was traveling to Fort Lewis, Washington, but would be stopping in Castro Valley for one night.

Raymond wanted me to meet his wife and two-year-old daughter. I drove over to Castro Valley to meet him and his family. Raymond introduced me to his wife, Rebecca, and his beautiful little daughter, Amy. Rebecca was pregnant with their second child. It was a great meeting and it was good to see that Raymond survived combat.

He then asked me for a favor. "Can you help me locate my parents, I have a lot of apologies to make to them," he said. I told him that I would do my best and I should have an answer by the end of the day. The plan was to meet at the Marie Callendar's restaurant in Castro Valley after my shift ended. I returned to my office at the police station and called everyone I could think of in an attempt to contact Raymond's parents. Apparently, his parents did not own a computer and they did not participate on any social media sites.

Then I had an idea! I knew that Raymond's dad was a master plumber so I contacted the plumbers union. I asked the secretary if she had a current listing for Bruce, the master plumber that once lived in Castro Valley. The nice lady was able to locate Bruce and Evelyn living in Redding California. I had found them!

I called dispatch and requested they contact the Redding Police Department and make a home visit to verify Bruce and Evelyn still lived at the listed address. About fifteen minutes later I received a call from Evelyn. I immediately recognized her voice, even though she was crying. She asked, "Is my son all right Officer Gill? Is he all right?" I told her that Raymond was fine and after a long conversation, with a lot of crying on her end, I updated her on her son's new life. I informed her that Raymond was on his way to report for duty at Fort Lewis, Washington, and that he wanted to see her and he wanted her to see her new granddaughter. She tearfully said, "Please give him our phone number. Please tell him to call because, I have really missed him."

Later that evening I met with Raymond and his family at Marie Callendar's as planned. We sat in a booth and I told Raymond that I had found his parents. I gave Raymond his parents' telephone number and address in Redding with the message "Your mother is waiting for you to call." Raymond took the telephone number and immediately called the number. It was tough to choke back tears when I saw a young combat veteran cry when he heard his mother's voice. It was a good reunion.

Raymond wanted to know what happened to his old friends from high school. Sadly, I had to tell Raymond that the news was not good. I started with the news about his friend, Keith. The three friends drank a lot of alcohol and they smoked a lot of weed but Keith eventually wanted to try heroin. He died of an overdose. Keith's parents had left him alone with the other two friends, Terry and Michael, so that they could spend the weekend in Lake Tahoe. When they returned home that Sunday night, they found Keith lying on the floor of their garage—the heroin needle till in his arm. Keith had died instantly of a drug overdose.

His friends Terry and Michael were with Keith and they ran from the garage when they saw Keith had died. They told investigators they ran because they were scared and "Keith, looked like he was dead."

Michael became a homeless alcoholic and was known around town as the "town drunk." He spent many nights in the Santa Rita jail's "drunk tank" and it was not uncommon to see him in alleys looking through dumpsters.

Terry could not find a full time job. He had numerous DUI arrests and lost his driver's license. Terry had many part time jobs but was not able to keep a job for long because he was a pot head. Terry was still living at home with his parents.

I ended the bad news saying, "Isn't it ironic that you had to go off to war to get away from your friends and that saved your life!" Raymond answered with, "Yes, and I plan on making the army my career and after my enlistment becoming a police officer."

I told Raymond that I would be happy to write a letter of recommendation should he decide to go into law enforcement.

The next morning, Raymond and his family were driving their rented U-Haul truck towards the freeway. I gave them a police escort to the freeway and as I entered the freeway on-ramp, I pulled over to the side of the road. As their truck passed my patrol car and entered the freeway I gave Raymond a military style salute to show respect.

Good job Raymond, and good luck!

Chapter 5

Nick's Big Mistake

About a year passed and I had been keeping up with Nick, and whenever I spoke with his principal, Jack, I was told Nick was doing well. Things were working out for Nick and Laura.

There was a convenience store near Nick's apartment, and I was told Nick was allowed to go there after school, after completing his homework, to play video games. The video game was in the front of the store, and the convenience store clerk knew Nick as a good kid who kept to himself.

The store clerk also knew about a group of kids who were always stealing from the store. They were in a gang that I called the Bonehead Gang.

One day the Boneheads stopped Nick as he was on his way

to the convenience store. They knew about Nick's dad and his dad's reputation. It appeared that Nick's dad was a gang member with a rough street reputation. They asked Nick if the stories about his dad were true. Nick answered "Yes," because he did not know what to say.

They told Nick that they had heard all about his father's fights with other gang members and his running from the police. They said he was "cool" and that Nick was lucky to have such a cool dad to look up to.

Then they told Nick they had a plan to steal beer and drink the beer at their gang clubhouse. They asked Nick if he was in, and Nick felt peer pressure to say yes.

Here was their simple plan. They knew Nick was allowed inside the convenience store. Nick was supposed to go inside the store and a couple of minutes later the gang members would enter and distract the clerk while Nick stole the beer. Nick agreed to help, but deep down he was scared.

Nick went inside the store as usual and began playing the video game. A couple of minutes later, the Boneheads walked inside the store. The clerk immediately became concerned, and he watched them walk to the rear of the store. Through the security mirrors mounted on the rear aisle wall, he watched them open and close the cooler doors. The five Boneheads were laughing and purposely acting suspicious. The clerk had the telephone in his hands because he just knew they were up to no good.

That's when Nick made his move. He walked over to a beer display near the front door. He grabbed a twelve-pack of beer and ran out the front door with it under his arm.

The store clerk was surprised at Nick, and he ran out of the store to catch him. The clerk forgot all about the five Boneheads at the rear of the store. That's when the five Boneheads grabbed large bags of potato chips and five more twelve-packs of beer.

The Boneheads ran in the opposite direction from the way Nick had run. The clerk was able to catch up with Nick several blocks away from the store, and he escorted Nick back to the convenience store to call the police. The clerk was very angry with Nick, as well as surprised about his actions. Nick had been going to the store for a long time, and the clerk trusted him.

I just happened to be in the area of the convenience store so I responded to the 911 calls made by the clerk. I was surprised to see Nick at the scene of the crime. "Are you a witness, Nick?" I asked, "Did you see the Boneheads who stole the beer? Tell me what you saw, Nick."

The clerk told me Nick was one of the thieves. Nick was a thief? There must be a mistake. Nick is not a Bonehead; Nick is a good kid. But Nick did not deny the clerk's claim that he was with the Boneheads that day. I had no choice but to take Nick into custody, thinking, This will break his mother's heart. She has been working hard to keep Nick out of trouble and away from the Boneheads in his neighborhood.

It was a long and quiet drive to Nick's apartment. What was I going to say to Nick's mom, Laura? What happened to Nick, and why did he steal the beer from the convenience store with the Boneheads? Maybe they threatened Nick if he did not help them steal the beer? There must be an answer. Why was Nick being so quiet about the trouble he was in?

Nick finally wanted to know the truth about his dad. "Is my dad a gang member like the Boneheads said? Where is he? What is the truth about my dad?"

Laura was very upset about the incident, but she finally told Nick all about his dad:"Yes, your dad is a gang member, and he is now doing time in prison for drug possession, auto theft, and strong-arm robbery." Laura told Nick that his dad had a bad street reputation with a lot of enemies looking for him. Laura told Nick she was afraid his dad's enemies were after them, so she had tried to keep his dad's life and crimes a secret.

Nick was angry with his mom, and I left them to talk, hoping that maybe Nick could get back on the right track. But Nick and

Laura would never be the same.

A couple of days later, while walking home from school, Nick ran into members of the Boneheads. They were happy to see Nick. They invited him over to the clubhouse to have some beer. Why not? I'm a thief like my dad, Nick thought.

Nick drank beer with his new gang-member friends, and he wanted to know more about being a good Bonehead gang member like his dad. Just maybe Nick could get a good reputation like his gang-member dad. Nick wanted to make his dad proud.

The Boneheads told Nick he had to be jumped into the gang if he wanted to join them. Nick agreed to the jump in, and five other gang members circled Nick and began to physically kick and beat him as part of the gang jump-in initiation ceremony.

After about fourteen seconds of a physical beating, Nick was officially in the gang. The new Bonehead gang member was ready to celebrate with his new crime partners. Stolen beer was passed around, and Nick was happy because he made his dad proud.

Nick did not go home that night because he had a lot of large bruises and marks on his body. Nick did not want to have to explain to his mother the suspicious bruises from the jump-in. He knew she would not approve of his decision to join the gang. Laura called the police to report Nick as a runaway when he did not return home that night.

Laura though Nick was angry with her for putting him on restriction for stealing the beer from the convenience store. But she was wrong about Nick that night.

Laura was lost and did not know how to help her son. Her baby Nick was gone.

Chapter 6

Nick's Bad Habits

One of the Boneheads had a cigarette habit, and he asked Nick if he knew how to smoke. Nick, of course, said, "Yes, I smoke all the time." That's when the Bonehead gave him a cigarette. Nick was nervous but up to the challenge.

Nick stood there with the cigarette between his fingers, and he watched the other place the cigarette and draw in the smoke. Nick said it had been a long time and that he had tried to quit; finally he put the cigarette to his lips and took a drag from the cigarette.

Nick began to cough and choke, just as everyone does when they smoke a cigarette for the first time in their life. All the Boneheads started to laugh and make fun of Nick. Nick tried to laugh it off, but the gang knew he had never smoked before. That was okay as far as the gang was concerned because Nick showed them that he had guts and was not afraid to try anything. Nick made it as far as the gang was concerned. The Boneheads took turns showing Nick how to smoke a cigarette.

Now that Nick was a smoker, he had to supply the gang with replacement cigarettes. The only way was to steal them, the way the other gang members did. Nick learned that the local grocery store received a cigarette shipment on Mondays and that the truck driver placed boxes and boxes of cigarettes near the store's employee break room and restroom area. Nick would ask to go to the restroom, and as he walked in that direction he would take a couple of cartons of cigarettes and place them in his backpack.

Because Nick figured out a way to get the gang cigarettes, he was seen as a hero. Nick could get cigarettes easy whenever he wanted to resupply the gang with smokes.

This went on for several weeks until the head grocery clerk suspected Nick was stealing from the store. She followed Nick into the break room and caught him stealing the cartons of cigarettes. Nick was putting the cigarettes in his backpack when the head clerk caught him. He dropped the backpack and tried to run, but one of the grocery load crewmembers stopped him before he could make his escape from the store.

Nick was escorted to the manager's office and the police were called. Nick was caught stealing again. But he was not afraid because he was making a reputation for himself to impress his gang.

Again Nick was arrested, and again Nick was placed on juvenile probation. Nick's reputation and rating with the gang grew. Nick's dad would be proud.

Chapter 7

A Family Reunited

Then one day Nick received a big surprise. Nick's dad, Oscar, was home on parole. Nick would finally meet the man he'd heard so much about. Nick was very excited.

Now Nick could get the full story right from the source, his dad. So much to learn and so much to experience! Wait until the gang heard that his dad was home from prison! Laura was not happy, but she did not know what to do.

There were no hugs or kisses from Oscar. Nick just stood there, staring at his dad. All Oscar wanted was a cold beer.

Oscar had a face that looked like cold stone, and his face and arms were tanned from the prison yard sun. Oscar had fresh prison tattoos on both arms. His body was in good physical shape from working out on the yard, and he wore his shirt prison-style, with only the top button attached.

Nick had a million questions for his dad, but he did not know where to start. Oscar was cold and standoffish, with a good prison stare. That made the homecoming uneasy.

Oscar made a phone call and left the apartment to take care of business. Laura knew what that meant. That meant Oscar was going out to get loaded on drugs. Laura knew Oscar would return later that night angry and violent. She did not want Nick to see his dad stoned and angry. Laura told Oscar to stay at his mother's house and not return to the apartment. Oscar's mother lived on the west side of town, far away from the apartment. That was fine with her.

Oscar was gone for three days, and Nick waited for his dad anxiously every night. Nick had questions. Lots of questions. Nick wanted to tell the boneheads about his dad's gang adventures in prison.

Finally, Nick cut school and spent time with his dad.

Oscar had lots of stories about life on the streets as a gang member, and lots of stories about life as a convicted felon. Nick was glued to every story.

Nick arranged for some of the Bonehead gang members to cut school too, and they came over to meet his dad. They were impressed to finally meet the gang member they heard so much about. Oscar had the floor, and all the little gangsters were listening to every word the OG (original gangster) had to say. He used words like respect, put in work for the gang, and watch each other's back. Oscar told them that is how you survive prison.

Oscar told them never to be a "rat" or a "snitch" and just keep your mouth shut if you see something in the joint. Being a rat was the worst. The young gangsters were being schooled in gang values. Nick was so proud to listen to his dad talk about the gangster lifestyle and explain the rules.

"Let's celebrate," one gangster said, and he pulled out a small bag of marijuana.

"That's not enough," another little gangster said, so a plan was made to walk down to the corner and rip off one of the local drug dealers.

Why not? We are the Boneheads! This is our turf! We don't ask for anything. We just take what we want!

Six Boneheads walked to the corner and roughed up one of the local drug dealers. They took his dope and his cash. They left their calling card by spray-painting their tag on the wall before they left the area.

They all partied until late into the night. Again Nick was so proud of his gang and his dad.

Chapter 8

Nick Learns about His Dad

It didn't take long for Oscar to begin hanging out with his old friends from his gang and from prison. Oscar forgot to see his parole officer, and he forgot to find a job, and he certainly forgot to not get stoned like he promised the prison parole board. Oscar was back to his old ways.

That's when it happened. Oscar and his old friend were driving around stoned when a police officer happened to recognize them as being a couple of parolees. The officer pulled up behind them to check them out, and Oscar remembered he was in possession of drugs. His friend was in possession of a stolen gun. What do we do? I know—let's try to outrun the police.

Now we have a police pursuit because they refused to stop.

Additional police cars joined in the pursuit, and now Oscar is preparing to run if and when his prison buddies stop the car. Looking for an escape route is on Oscar's mind right now. Not his promise to change once outside prison, not his wife Laura, and certainly not his son Nick. Running and escaping the police are the only things on Oscar's mind.

Four police cars, lights and sirens blaring, were chasing them and Oscar was set to run. The buddy lost control of the car and crashed into a parked car.

That did not stop Oscar. He sprang his door open and took off like a gazelle. Oscar was running in the night, trying to escape the police. He was jumping over fences and putting some distance between himself and the pursuing officers.

He was doing pretty well until he heard the bark of the police dog. He had to hide and try to lose the dog. Just then, Oscar saw an apartment carport with a large van parked in it.

Oscar climbed onto the roof of the van, and he decided to try to squeeze into a small space and hide. The police dog was near, so Oscar kept very quiet.

The dog stopped and made a circle around the parked van. Oscar's scent was somewhere around the van. The police officer who was the dog's handler shined his flashlight around the parked van because his dog was indicating that there was no more adrenaline from the runner. The runner must be around here.

Soon other officers arrive, and they began shining their flashlights as well. Suddenly one officer happened to see the sole of Oscar's shoe on the roof of the van.

"Come on down!" they yelled at Oscar. "We see you up there! Show us your hands!" Now all the flashlights were shining on Oscar.

I guess the chase was over. With great reluctance Oscar yelled out, "Okay! Don't shoot!" He slowly climbed down to the ground and was placed in handcuffs.

It was a good night. A good police pursuit, the police dog did his job, and two prison parolees were captured and on their way back to prison.

Now Oscar would meet his parole officer in jail. Oscar was in jail for three days when his parole hearing was held. Oscar came up with several lies to give to the parole board, but they did not buy into any of them. Oscar had failed to check in with his parole officer, he had failed to find a job, and his mandatory urinalyses indicated the presence of marijuana and methamphetamine in his system. Oscar was on his way back to state prison. Nick got the word, and he was heartbroken.

Laura decided to move so that Nick would get away from the Boneheads and get a fresh start.

Chapter 9

Nick is Not a Good Example

Nick couldn't help himself. He was lost without the Boneheads, so he tried to entertain himself with some of the stories his dad had told him about.

One day before school Nick was walking with Jason, a kid who lived in his new apartment building. Jason was very naive and easily led astray by streetwise Nick.

Nick had an idea: let's play basketball in the apartment complex before school. Jason was confused, but he followed Nick's lead .Nick took the basketball and bounced the ball against the doors and walls inside the apartment complex. A few people who were home would come to the door and say, "Hey, kid, stop bouncing that ball against the wall of my apartment!" If no one was in the apartment, Nick knew it was empty and could take the service alley behind the apartment to look for an open window.

On the first day, Nick found an open bathroom window to an apartment. Jason was small, so Nick helped him up and pushed him through the open window. "Just go around and open the front door for me," said Nick.

Jason made it to the living room and opened the front door for Nick. "Let's look for cash, alcohol and guns," said Nick.

Jason saw a large video collection near the big-screen TV, and he started looking for karate videos. He was excited to find some videos he wanted to watch. He began placing the videos in his school backpack. Nick found a small amount of cash in the master bedroom, but soon he too began to have a good time finding karate videos like Jason.

Suddenly they heard something near the front door. It was the apartment owner, back from the store. Nick and Jason have to leave. "Let's go out the bathroom window because the way out is closed off. Hurry! The owner is getting closer."

Nick was quickly out through the window and Jason is only seconds behind him. The two boys ran to school. They got away with it.

Just as Jason walked onto the school lawn, terror struck him. "Nick! I forgot my backpack on the living room floor!" Jason cried. "We're doomed."

Nick told Jason not to snitch if called to the principal's office. "Just tell them you lost the backpack on your way to school."

The apartment renter called the police to report someone had broken into his apartment and ransacked his bedroom. The owner noticed forty-three dollars missing from his dresser, and he located the backpack on the floor in front of his TV. When the police arrived, the officer took possession of the backpack. Inside the backpack was the apartment owner's CDs, a school lunch, and Jason's homework.

I got the call to meet the beat officer at the apartment complex. He gave me the backpack to take to the elementary school. I drove over to the elementary school and spoke with the principal, Jim Freeland. I gave him a brief explanation of the prior call and asked him if he had a student on campus named Jason.

A computer check listed Jason's address as the same address as the apartment that was broken into. Jim also told me Jason had been hanging out with Nick and that Nick was a problem student. A computer check revealed that Nick also lived in the same apartment complex.

The principal said it was easy to get the truth out of Jason, but Nick was going to be hard. I was familiar with Nick, so we called Jason to the principal's office.

Little Jason came in and his eyes were wide and scared. I started out telling Jason, "I know what you and Nick did this morning before school."

It didn't take long; right away Jason started to cry uncontrollably. He said, "It was all Nick's idea."

The principal asked Jason, "What was Nick's idea?"

Jason gave us the whole story. It was Nick who used the basketball to bounce off the walls and doors in order to tell who was home, and it was Nick who located the open window in the alley.

After letting Jason calm down, Jim called Nick to his office. Nick was different and harder to break. Nick had been in trouble before, and he knew the rules. Never snitch or turn rat. Nick was going to be harder to break.

Principal Freeland had no patience with Nick. He asked Nick why he broke into the apartment with Jason. Nick denied everything. Principal Freeland said he was going to suspend Nick from school because he and Jason had broken into an apartment on their way to school. Nick was very defiant, and challenged Freeland about his authority to suspend him from school.

Principal Freeland called Jason's mother and Nick's mother

Laura, and requested that they come to school to take their sons home on suspension. Nick remained defiant, so I decided to transport him to the police station for court processing. Nick showed no emotions about going to the police station.

At the police station I spoke with Laura regarding Nick. She told me she was at her wits' end because Nick was out of control. She had caught him sneaking out of the apartment several times late at night, and she suspected he had been smoking and drinking. She told me that when she confronted him, Nick would deny everything and call her crazy.

I gave Laura the names of a group of adolescent guidance counselors and a list of drug and alcohol counselors. I called Nick into the office and told him that he had to attend counseling and he would not be monitored by me every day. Laura looked helpless; she knew she had her hands full with Nick the rebel.

Chapter 10

Nick the Artist

Nick was a very talented artist. If only he could direct his energy to that discipline! As I patrolled my beat every Monday, I would travel the alleys to look for graffiti. If I found any, I would notify the property owner and take photos of the graffiti. I would then take the photos to art teachers at the high school and ask if they recognized the work. Many times they immediately recognized the student artist and I would call them to my office at school and arrange for them and their parents to clean up their graffiti.

One day, I located new graffiti on the back wall of a drugstore on my beat. The graffiti was a man's face, and it was very pronounced because I could see the wrinkles on the image. Good work—but it was still illegal. I thought someone had taken a lot of time painting this graffiti because if was very detailed. Who was this new graffiti artist?

My question went unanswered for weeks before I got a break. Nick was caught at school drawing graffiti, and I met with him and the assistant principal to discuss the incident at school. Nick admitted drawing graffiti on a locker near the maintenance yard. The assistant principal searched Nick's backpack and discovered photos of more graffiti. One photo was the image of the man's face from the back of the drugstore's wall.

Nick admitted that it was his art, and he and his mother agreed to clean up his work. I did not hear from Nick about graffiti for a while—until I got a call to meet an angry mother at the local hospital.

The mother said her twelve-year-old son had received a tattoo that was infected. She wanted the tattoo artist to be arrested. I asked the boy how he received that tattoo, and was told Nick had a tattoo gun and was giving tattoos in his garage.

I immediately went to Nick's house, and as I walked up the driveway I could hear voices from the garage. I could also hear the sound of a small engine. I walked to the side of the garage and saw the side door was open. Inside the garage I saw about ten boys, all teenagers, waiting for their tattoos.

Sitting at a small table were Nick and a fairly large thirteen-year-old boy. Nick was tattooing the word Moose on his arm. Everyone stopped when I entered the garage.

The first thing I said was, "What are you doing? And where are your parents?"

Nick immediately responded, saying, "It okay, OG, they all want tattoos." That was the first time Nick referred to me as OG (for "Officer Gill"). Soon all the kids at school would greet me as OG.

I instructed Nick to stop all tattoos now and get his mother here now. I told Nick one of his tattoo subjects was in the hospital receiving a tetanus shot for a possible infection. I also told him the mother of the boy wanted to sue his mother for his handiwork.

I took the names of all the boys in the garage and called their parents before sending them home. I took a look at the tattoo gun and saw it was a crude prison-type tattoo gun. Nick's dad had showed him how to make it.

The tattoo gun had a motor taken from a toy car, a cylinder from a fountain pen, and a sewing machine needle, and it was pieced together with low-grade wire. Nick was using ink from a fountain pen, and none of the equipment was sterile.

While waiting for Moose's parents, I took a photo of the tattoo and realized Nick had not done a bad job. Too bad it was all illegal.

I informed Nick that to be a tattoo artist he had to be licensed by the state and had to receive a permit for the Health Department. Finally I told Nick he could not tattoo anyone under eighteen years old unless a parent or legal guardian signed for the tattoo.

The parents worked things out and everyone was happy with the final outcome. What's next, Nick?

Chapter 11

Nick Continues his Evil Ways

Well, it didn't take long before Nick was back to his evil ways. He was on juvenile probation, and his probation officer had problems. Nick had a curfew, which he often violated. Nick had to attend school on a regular schedule, which he rarely did. Nick had to attend alcohol and Al-anon meetings on a monthly basis, which he refused to do.

Nick's probation officer threatened to place him in juvenile hall on the weekends, but that had no effect on Nick. It appeared that Nick was working to get a street reputation. Going to juvenile hall could help him get that reputation. I'm sure that would make his dad proud.

Nick had a charisma about him, and a lot of kids wanted to

hang out with him even though (or maybe because) they knew his reputation. Nick was not allowed to hang out with Jason anymore, so he had a new friend who lived down the street. The new friend's name was Peter.

Peter was from a broken home. Peter's mom and dad were much older, and they did not understand Peter's generation. His dad lived in another city, and sometimes he would visit Peter on the weekends. Peter's mother had no interest in her son, and she often reminded him that his birth was an accident and a big mistake. Peter just gravitated toward Nick because Nick showed interest in him.

Nick always had a scheme or a con on his mind. This time, Nick wanted to break into homes, so they armed themselves with hot dogs. Nick or Peter would take turns knocking on the front door of a home. If there was no answer, they would go to the backyard and look for a doggie door. If they saw a dog, they would throw the dog a piece of hot dog. Soon the dog would allow Nick or Peter to enter the residence through the doggie door.

Nick or Peter would then open the front door for the other, and they would take turns feeding hot dogs to the dog while the other one searched the home for cash, alcohol, or guns. They had backpacks to carry their loot because no one suspected school kids. Instead of going to school, Nick and Peter would break into homes during school hours.

Their plan went well until one day a LOL (little old lady) saw them loitering around when they should be in class. She called the police and as they walked down the street, a police officer stopped them.

While he was detaining them, the officer learned that the boys were a couple of blocks from their school and he decided to drive them there. His assumption was that he was detaining truants from school. The officer asked the boys if they were in possession of anything dangerous, and he searched the boys and their backpacks.

That's when he discovered an unopened bottle of beer in one of the backpacks. Peter broke right away and told the officer where the beer had come from. Nick remained silent and defiant the entire time. Nick knew his rights, and he remained silent.

Chapter 12

Nick Meets a Girl

For a couple of months after that incident, Nick had stayed out of trouble, and he was trying to take the right road when he saw her at school. She was beautiful and he was interested in her right away. Nick wondered: What was her name? Was she new to the school? Why had I not seen her before? How could I meet her? What should I say?

Her name was Lisa, and she was not new at Nick's school. Maybe Nick had been so busy being cool around his gang-member friends that he didn't notice her before. But now Nick wanted to meet her.

There was a small group of girls interested in bad boys, so maybe they knew Lisa, he thought. One girl had a class with

Lisa, and Nick asked her a lot of questions about Lisa. What was she like?

Lisa was from a very strict home with a big brother named Carl who was very protective of his little sister. The big brother was on the school's football team, and he did not like anyone bothering his little sister. Nick learned that Carl was a senior and his little sister a freshman in high school. That did not bother Nick. He had to meet her, and he was willing to risk bodily harm to do it.

Nick got her schedule, and if he worked it right he would bump into her at school. Maybe she would see him and they could just talk. Nick was hoping to just get lucky and say hello to her.

After weeks of trying to be noticed by Lisa and after weeks of hoping and plotting, Nick almost gave up; but then it happened. Lisa noticed Nick, and the two said "Hi."

It was a start. Nick was so happy he did not know how to control himself.

Nick was on his way to class during passing period when Lisa was approaching him with a couple of her friends. Suddenly Lisa accidentally dropped her books and binder. Papers went all over the hallway, so of course Nick volunteered to help her get her papers so she would not be late for class. Nick was her hero. They shared eye contact, and that's all it took. Lisa wanted to know more about Nick.

At the end of school, Nick was waiting for his gang-member friends when Lisa approached him to talk. She wanted to thank him again for helping her in the hallway with her books and binders. Nick ignored his gang-member friends because he wanted to walk Lisa home and just talk to her. Here was his chance to meet the girl he had been seeing for weeks at school!

The whole school noticed Nick and Lisa together. What would her big brother Carl think when he learned that his little sister was walking and talking with that gangbanger, loser kid named Nick? Could there be an after-school fight in the works?

The next day rumors began to spread about Lisa and Nick walking together after school. What would Lisa's big brother do about Nick? Lisa might get the wrong reputation if she was seen with that loser kid, Nick. Something had to be done.

Carl was angry, and his football friends wanted to know what he was going to do about Nick and his sister Lisa. Carl told his friends that he planned on fighting Nick if he caught them together. Carl did not want his little sister to get a reputation as being a girl who hung around gang members at school. A fight would occur if things didn't change, and quickly. The school rumor mill was in full swing now. School fight between Carl and Nick!

Nick ignored the schoolyard rumors because he wanted to see Lisa again. Nick's gang-member friends wanted to know if he planned on taking on Carl, because Carl was now doing a lot of bold talk about fighting Nick. Both boys had a reputation to uphold.

Then it happened. It was the end of another school day, and Nick was supposed to meet Lisa at their spot to walk home. Carl heard about the spot, and he and his football friends went to confront Nick. Nick's gang-member friends heard about the football players headed toward Nick and Lisa, and they decided to go there too in order to back up Nick.

All the ingredients for a school fight.

Nick's friends got to the spot first. One gang member had a knife, and he offered the knife to Nick for protection. At first Nick declined the knife, but his friends insisted because Carl was a football player with a lot of big football-player friends. Lisa did not know what was going on and she was confused. Lisa thought, Why is Nick friends with these loser gang members?

Then it all came together when Lisa saw her brother Carl with his football team members approaching. Nick quickly took the knife. "Maybe I'll just show Carl the knife and he will back down." That was a good plan—right.

A large crowd began to gather to see the fight. Carl and Nick were going to go at it. This was going to be a good after-school fight. A football player versus a gang member! The whole school would be talking about this fight for weeks.

But it wasn't going to happen this day, because the football coach learned about the fight. The coach couldn't have any of his players suspended because of a school fight.

The coach alerted the school administrators, and the administrators alerted the SRO.

As soon as the kids spotted the school administrators, everyone began to scatter. Some students told what was going on as school administrators stopped them. It was a fight between Carl, the football player, and that troublemaking kid Nick.

An administrator caught up with Carl and Lisa and escorted them to the main office. Nick and his friends were seen walking fast away from the school. I caught up with Nick in my patrol car. I called him by name and he stopped immediately. His friends did not stop, and they did not look back to see if their friend Nick was all right. That's a gang member for you; get away at all costs and only think about yourself if stopped by the police.

I told Nick he had to return to school, and that I would give him a ride back in the patrol car. Nick stood by the patrol-car door and just waited. I told Nick that I had to search him before allowing him inside my car, and that's when I felt a large pocketknife in his right pocket.

"Is that a knife, Nick?" Nick did not answer the question. I reached in the pocket and pulled out a large Buck-type folding pocketknife. "Are you carrying a knife now, Nick?" Again Nick did not answer. He knew his rights, and he refused to answer any questions from the police.

Nick and I returned to the administrator's office because the administrators wanted to collect Nick's side of the fight story.

By now the administrators had learned about the Carl and Lisa side of the story, but Nick refused to talk. The school administrator had no other choice but to suspend Nick with a recommendation for an expulsion from school because of having a knife on campus.

When the administrator was done, I transported Nick to the police station to process him for possession of a dangerous weapon at school. The entire time Nick did not talk about the knife or who was responsible for having the knife at school— just like a good little gang member. The truth would have been good to hear for a change.

Chapter 13

Nick's New School

Nick was expelled from the regular high school for one year and sent to the alternative high school. He continued refusing to tell how he came to be in possession of a pocketknife, and he refused to inform on his gang. Nick had a lot of other people to blame for his mistakes. According to him, everyone was against him and everyone is to blame. Poor blameless Nick! Everyone was out to get him and everyone was against him.

On his first day at the alternative high school, Ashley zeroed in on him. Ashley liked bad boys, and she'd heard all about bad boy Nick.

Ashley came from a dysfunctional home, and she needed attention. Her mother was an alcoholic; her father was an alcoholic and a racist bigot.

Nick was the perfect way for Ashley to make her father angry because he was a minority kid, and her father would blow his lid when he learned she was interested in a gangbanging minority bad boy. Ashley was ready to help Nick enter his new school.

Nick had no idea what was about to happen to him. Being a new kid at a new school was challenging because other groups were claiming the campus. First Nick had to meet the principal and learn the new rules.

The new principal, Mr. Warner, was a veteran administrator who had heard all about Nick before he walked on the campus. Warner did not judge Nick, but he was prepared to let Nick know he was not going to tolerate any of Nick's gang nonsense.

Principal Warner had 168 student misfits on campus, with all sorts of personal issues. Some had attendance problems, authority issues, and disciplinary problems. He had substance abusers, drug dealers, taggers, goth students, heavy-metal students, black power students, mentally disturbed students, loners, and gang members who opposed Nick's gang. Warner had a Cracker Jack group of misfits, all of whom needed an education. Yes, he had his hands full, and the rules were strictly enforced.

Warner was not alone; he had a full-time juvenile probation officer assigned to the school. Over half the students were on probation, and some were wards of the juvenile court.

Nick had to follow the rules or get kicked out of another school and violate his new probation. As Nick waited to see his new principal, trouble came his way.

A student named Jason was sent to the office on a disciplinary referral from a teacher. He and Nick locked eyes on each other. Not a word was said between Jason and Nick, but they made each other uncomfortable by just staring at each other. I'm sure Nick would have felt better if one of his homeboys had been on campus to back him up.

The street term for that look is "mean mugging each other."

The school secretary, Judy, knew the look, and she called the principal on the telephone to come out and deal with the two boys.

Warner quickly laid the hammer down on Jason and laid down the rules. The teacher in class had the final say and was in charge of the classroom. Jason had to keep his mouth shut and learn. Warner sent Jason back to class; and now it was Nick's turn to see his new principal.

Warner told Nick in no uncertain terms that this was his chance to prove himself so he could return to the regular high school and graduate. Warner told Nick to stop his foolish behavior and settle down because only he, Nick, could do it. Warner also told Nick that because the campus was smaller, all staff and his probation officer would closely watch him.

Nick left the office to see his first teacher on his first day. At that moment Ashley approached him again. She had been waiting for him to leave the principal's office. Ashley had a lot to tell Nick, and she loved attention from her new bad boyfriend. Ashley had heard the principal's speech many times, and she told Nick not to worry because they all got the same speech.

Ashley asked Nick if he had cigarettes, or anything else to smoke, because she had a spot off campus for smoking. Nick told her no, so she said, "If I can score some weed, do you want to leave and get high?" Nick again did the right thing and told her that this was his first day at school, so he wanted to stay sober.

Ashley was spotted by her teacher and told to report to her classroom. Ashley told Nick to meet up with her later and they could get high together. Nick realized Ashley was a risk taker, and she was out to get him into trouble. How could he stay clean at school?

It was break time and Nick was on his way to the school courtyard. Warner and James, the assigned probation officer, were watching the students when they both noticed something odd. Suddenly all the students were headed to the courtyard. Something was about to happen. Nick did not notice anything wrong, but Jason told students that he was going to "box" Nick. Everyone wanted to see the fight.

As Nick drew closer to the center of the courtyard, Jason approached him with a fight on his mind. Nick was totally surprised. Jason said, "Check yourself, fool!" and without another word took a swing at Nick. Nick was able to dodge the punch, and he pushed Jason back.

Lucky for Nick, Principal Warner and Probation Officer James Coleman happened to see Jason threaten Nick. They broke up the disturbance and sent students back to class. Jason and Nick were escorted to the principal's office for their official hearing. Jason admitted that he wanted to fight Nick because he'd heard about his gang reputation on the streets. Nick said he had no idea what reputation Jason was talking about.

Warner suspended Jason from school for causing a disturbance, and Probation Officer Coleman said Jason had violated his juvenile probation. Back to juvenile hall and classes in custody for Jason. Warner recommended that Nick go home for the day so that Warner could calm his campus. Nick thought that was not fair to him, but he went home at the urging of his principal and probation officer. It was again clear to Nick that everyone was against him.

Chapter 14

Nick Goes to a Party

Ashley threw a party. Her parents had left her home unsupervised while they went to Lake Tahoe for the weekend. That was their first mistake. The second was them thinking she would stay home alone all weekend.

It didn't take long; soon after they left, Ashley called many of her school friends. Nick was one of the first calls she made, to make sure he got the official word of the party.

Nick had a curfew, but he was sure he could trick his mother and probation officer to attend the party of the year. Nick did not want to go by himself, so he invited his gang homeboys. Maybe Ashley would be interested in one of them and she would give Nick a break with all her advances and offers. Ashley could be a dangerous girl because she was always asking him to leave campus and get high.

There were many students at Ashley's house when Nick and his homeboys arrived. Or Nick thought they were students. They could have been students. Maybe former students? Maybe future students? Maybe students from other schools? Nick and his homeboys saw a lot of young people from all over the area. I guess a lot of people got the word out that Ashley was having a party.

When they walked into the house, everyone was drinking or smoking or just trying to dance to the extremely loud music. Now, this was a party!

Suddenly Ashley spotted Nick. She ran over and gave him a big hug and a kiss. Ashley was happy to see Nick; now she could act out her plan to get to know the real bad boy.

Ashley gave Nick a beer and asked him if he wanted to see her room. Nick was suspicious of Ashley, but he said, "Yeah, sure," only because his homeboys were listening. They thought Nick was a player because he had this hot girl asking him to see her room.

The two went upstairs, but the trip was slow because of all the people crowded into the house. The stairs were occupied by a lot of people just standing around talking and listening to the loud music.

Finally they arrived at Ashley's bedroom. Ashley was excited to show Nick her bedroom, but the room was occupied by some of her friends. One of Ashley's friends from school was in the room with her boyfriend. They wanted to be alone.

Ashley offered to show Nick her parents' bedroom. The door was closed and she had told everyone at the party that the master bedroom was off-limits.

They went into the master bedroom, and finally they were alone. The room was big as Nick looked around. Ashley started hugging and kissing Nick; but then suddenly the police were at the front door. The neighbors had called about the loud music coming from the house. Ashley told Nick to wait while she went to talk to the police. She nervously left the bedroom to go to the front door.

As Ashley went downstairs, she could hear her guests quickly leaving the house because they did not want to deal with the police. Could it be they were too young to drink alcohol? Or they were too young to smoke? Or just too young to be out so late? Everyone had their own reason to leave the party.

Nick was upstairs, trapped, because he had listened to Ashley. He was in the master bedroom of the home of total strangers. How do I get out of this house? he wondered. Nick decided to hide in the master bedroom closet until Ashley returned. That's when he saw the gun safe. What could be in a gun safe?

Nick grabbed the handle to the gun safe, and it was open. Wow, guns were in the gun safe! Ashley's father was a gun collector.

Nick saw a handgun on the shelf, so he picked it up to get a better look at it. It was a .45 caliber semiautomatic handgun, just like the ones seen in the movies. Nick took the magazine out and saw it was loaded. He pulled the slide back, like in the movies, and saw that it had a live round of ammunition in the slide. Wow, the gun was fully loaded! Nick put the loaded handgun in his waistband because he had always wanted a gun. Now he had one.

Now Nick had a new dilemma: how to leave the room and get out of the house with his stolen handgun. With all the confusion and the quick exiting by all the partygoers, he saw his moment to make a clean getaway.

Nick was able to get downstairs, and he left the house through the sliding glass door in the family room. He climbed over the back fence, and he was on the road on his way back home with a loaded handgun in his waistband. What was he going to do with this gun? He had to find a place to hide it.

Nick couldn't take it home because his mother might find it and freak out. Nick couldn't give it to one of his homeboys because they might freak out as well. Nick was on probation and he'd just committed a felony. Should he take the gun back and put it in the gun safe? No, he couldn't go back because the police were there.

As Nick quickly walked home, he passed his school. I know, he thought, I'll put the stolen handgun in my locker at school. That is the perfect hiding place. The school did not have a fence, so it was easy to walk onto campus from the street. What a good idea—his locker at school.

Once Nick placed the stolen handgun in his school locker, he felt a little calmer. Now he could sneak back inside his house and go to his room as if nothing had ever happened. He'd gotten away with a perfect crime.

The next morning Nick was curious about what had happened after Ashley's party. Nick called his homeboys to find out if the police had made any arrest at the party. He learned that the police were too busy dealing with two girls who had been sick on the front lawn at the party. So Nick had a lucky break during his getaway. He also learned that Ashley's parents were called and told to return home from Lake Tahoe. Ashley was in a lot of trouble with both the police and her parents. Nick thought it was good he was able to get away because he was on probation with a curfew.

On Monday at school, everyone was talking about Ashley's party. The word was all over school. Ashley had a blowout party that took the entire police department to break up. The police made many arrests and called a lot of parents. A lot of kids were in trouble. Wow, what a weekend! Nick was lucky that he left the party when he did.

Nick went to his school locker, and it was still there—the stolen handgun from Ashley's house. Nick didn't touch it or stare at it long; he just wanted to see it again. Now he was in possession of real power. He wanted to tell one of his homeboys, but he knew it was better to keep it a secret for now. How long could Nick keep his little secret?

Nick nervously went to class, heavy with the knowledge that he had a loaded handgun in his school locker. Nick also wondered where Ashley was. She was not on campus yet. Was she in juvenile hall? What happened when her parents made it home? The better question was: Did her father notice his handgun was missing from the gun safe? Nick began to worry more and more, not knowing what had happened to Ashley.

After Nick's third-period class he noticed a police car in the parking lot. What was going on? Why were the police here at school? Was he in trouble again? Did the police know that he stole a loaded handgun from Ashley's house? Nick was very curious about that police car.

Nick went to the principal's office and asked the principal's secretary, Judy, about the police car. Judy said she did not know, and Nick should go back to class. Nick knew she was not telling him the truth. Something was up, and he wondered what he should do about the handgun in his locker. He couldn't get caught with a gun.

Nick thought Ashley had told her father that he had been in the master bedroom and that he had taken the handgun from the gun safe.

Nick was thinking he should just go to the locker and take the gun off campus before the police found it. How could he sneak the gun off campus? Someone would see him; so he needed to be very careful. When should he do it? Now? He needed to do something before he got into trouble. Nick was deep in thought.

Nick made up his mind. He had to get the gun off campus. When everyone returns to class at the bell, he thought, I'm going to make my move. Nick waited around his locker until he heard the class bell ring. Soon the hall was clear and no one was around. Now was the time to make his big move.

Nick put the handgun in his backpack, and off he went. A teacher just happened to see Nick leaving the campus, and she called Judy, the principal's secretary. Judy walked over to the principal's office and told him Nick was seen leaving campus.

I was on campus, because I was the one who had driven the parked patrol car Nick had seen. I was just on campus to visit and had no other official business. Principal Warner told me about Ashley's party and that he had not received a call from Ashley's parents excusing her from school.

Principal Warner asked me to stop Nick and return him to his office to discuss his leaving school without an official pass. I drove in Nick's direction and slowly pulled up behind him. I could tell I'd caught him by surprise because of the surprised look in his eyes. Nick did not run; he just stood there like a statue.

I caught up to Nick less than two blocks from school. "Nick, where are you going?" I asked him.

His response was, "I need to go home because I don't feel good." Nick knew the rules required him to get a home pass and that the principal would call his mother to check in with her. Nick had followed none of the rules, so something was up. He had a nervous expression, and he looked around like he was going to run. I've seen that look before; Nick had the "escape look" in his eyes.

I decided to get out of the patrol car and approach Nick to see if doing so made his nervous look more pronounced — a sign of stress. I could almost see his heart beating out of his chest. Knowing Nick as I did, I was sure something was wrong.

"Nick, you broke the rules and I have to take you back to school," I said."Mr. Warner saw you leaving campus."

I told Nick to get into the patrol car. He complied, and as he started to enter the backseat, I grabbed his backpack. "You know I always search backpacks before I put someone in my patrol car." When I grabbed the backpack, it felt heavy. I asked Nick, "What's in your backpack, bricks?" Nick did not respond.

I searched the backpack, and the first thing I saw was a Colt 1911 (Gold Cup).45-caliber semiautomatic handgun. The handgun was an expensive collector's-edition firearm. I took the magazine out of the handle and saw the gun was loaded with a live round in the chamber.

I told Nick, "Now you are in big trouble. You had a handgun on campus." Nick was a good little gang member and did not say a word.

I placed the handgun in the trunk of my patrol car and drove Nick back to his school. Principal Warner was surprised to see Nick, and I informed him that Nick had been in possession of a loaded handgun on campus and that the handgun was now evidence locked inside my patrol car's trunk.

Principal Warner asked Nick if he had planned to shoot anyone on campus today. Nick said no. Then Nick was asked how he came to possess a loaded handgun, and Nick said, "It's not mine. I found it and I was taking it off campus." The more he answered, the more we could tell he was lying.

I went to my patrol car to get the registration number so that I could run the number for the registered owner, while Warner called Nick's mother to inform her of Nick's new legal problem.

The registered owner was Stan King, Ashley's father. I called Mr. King and informed him that I was in possession of his registered handgun and that the gun would be placed in evidence at the police station.

Mr. King informed me that his daughter had thrown a party over the weekend and the handgun must have been stolen during the party. I instructed Mr. King to escort his daughter Ashley to the police station so that I could further investigate the theft.

When I told Principal Warner that the handgun was stolen from Ashley's house and that her father owned the gun, Nick overheard my conversation, and he agreed to tell the truth about how he came into possession of a stolen handgun.

I read Nick his Miranda rights and Nick admitted that he was at Ashley's house during the party. He also admitted having taken the gun from Ashley's father's gun safe.

Nick came clean. Principal Warner overheard Nick's confession, and he had no choice but to suspend Nick. He immediately called Nick's probation officer and informed him of the latest Nick drama. I informed Nick that I had no choice but to book him into juvenile hall for felony grand theft of a handgun and felony possession of a loaded handgun at school.

Chapter 15

Nick's Mother Turns Him In

One day after school Laura, Nick's mother, was at the police station looking for me. She had a black briefcase that belonged to Nick.

I escorted her to a private office and she opened the briefcase. Inside were small plastic baggies with marijuana in each baggie. We started counting the baggies and ended up with thirty-four baggies filled with marijuana for sale.

Included in the briefcase was $365 in cash (all in five- and ten-dollar bills); a small scale; forty empty plastic baggies; a list of marijuana customers, including their telephone numbers; and a large Rambo-style knife. Laura told me her son Nick was selling marijuana at school. She said she found the briefcase in

Nick's closet when she was gathering his clothing to do laundry. Laura wanted me to arrest Nick when he made it home from school.

Just as I learned Nick was on his way home from school, Nick called his mother to get a ride home. Laura agreed to pick him up and deliver him instead to the police station. About ten minutes later, Laura and Nick were waiting in the police station lobby for me to arrest him. I escorted Laura and Nick to a private office to collect his statement.

The first thing Nick saw was his black briefcase, with all the contraband inside. Nick looked at his mother and she said, "I found that in your closet and I know what you are doing—you are selling drugs at school."

Before I could read Nick his Miranda rights, he admitted that he sold marijuana at school, but was doing it only to buy a car. Laura was so angry with Nick that she left the police station crying. I took Nick's statement and processed him for juvenile hall.

The next day I met with Assistant Principal Green, and I shared with him Nick's telephone book showing all of his marijuana customers.

The assistant principal and all the campus supervisors conducted a school locker search, and all the students on Nick's customer list were interviewed. I was asked to assist in the interviews of all the students. It was a long morning. Their parents were contacted and all involved students were suspended for marijuana use.

Nick was in juvenile hall and out of business, and students were looking over their shoulders to see if I was coming after them.

Chapter 16

Nick Meets Victor

Nick was released from juvenile hall on a very strict probation. He was not allowed to go out or stay out with permission, not allowed to miss one day of school, not allowed to socialize with his homeboys, and most of all required to obey all rules and laws. If he failed to obey the rules he would have to serve five years in the California Youth Authority (CYA) prison camp for juveniles. If sent to CYA, Nick could serve time until he was twenty-five years old. Nick was given a last chance to prove himself.

Nick was happy to be back home, but he had a hard time adjusting to not being in juvenile hall. When in the hall every decision was made for him, and all he had to do was listen for the bell to ring. When you hear the bell, it's time to get up and out of your cell. When you hear the bell, it's time to go to the restroom and get ready for breakfast. When you hear the bell, it's time to march for breakfast. When you hear the bell, it's time to clean up the mess hall after breakfast. When you hear the bell, it's time to march to class and go to school. Everything is set to the bell system, and you know your routine.

The only thing that was not routine was Nick's new gambling habit. When you are locked up all the time with kids from all over the state, you tend to pickup bad habits. Gambling was Nick's new habit. Nick learned how to play cards, dominos, and dice. Nick was good, but he also learned how to cheat at gambling. That could cause a problem if you get caught.

Nick could not wait to show his homeboys what he'd learned in juvenile hall. Nick was not allowed to hang with the homeboys, and he was not allowed to cheat at cards. Still, he reasoned, you can't get into trouble if you don't get caught. Nick was not planning on getting caught.

It didn't take long for his homeboys to learn he was out, and they had to celebrate his freedom. The homeboys planned a big get-together to hear the latest happenings from the hall.

Nick knew the rules, but he did not want to worry his mother so he told her he had a job interview. Finding a lawful job was one of the terms of his probation. His mother bought his story, so his first lie was very successful. Nick's mother was easy to fool.

Nick was doing well with his new skill at cards when he met the newest member of the Boneheads gang: Victor, a.k.a. Flaco. Victor was a brash and cocky young gangbanger who wanted to prove his toughness. Victor was ready to fight at the drop of a hat, and he had a large chip on his shoulder.

Nick and Victor took an instant dislike to each other, maybe because they were pretty much alike. Nick was unable to change Victor's mind about things, and both were determined to be in the right, no matter at what cost. Nick thought Victor was disrespectful around him because Nick had done time in juvenile hall, which meant he had earned respect. Victor gave no one respect.

Nick was teaching the gang a lesson in cards when Victor challenged him after a big loss. Victor did not like to lose at anything, and he especially did not like losing to Nick. Nick did not like being challenged by anyone, so the two began to argue. The argument escalated to a challenge to fight, so a fight was the only way to settle the argument. They made an agreement to meet in the "tunnel."

The tunnel was a railroad tunnel near the school. It was remote and quiet, and fights were pretty common there. Nick and Victor left the clubhouse to prepare for the big fight.

Victor was seen walking to the tunnel by several witnesses who wanted to see the fight between Nick and Victor. This was going to be a good fight!

It was a rainy day, and Victor had an open umbrella as he walked along the railroad track. Victor had his music headset on, and he was seen smoking a blunt. The open umbrella was intended to conceal his smoking marijuana. Victor did not notice the fast-approaching passenger train behind him. Witnesses saw Victor casually walking toward the tunnel, not knowing he was in serious danger.

Suddenly Victor stopped because he felt the vibrations on the railroad tracks. The train conductor was sounding the train horn, but because Victor was listening to his music headset he did not hear the loud train horn behind him.

Victor turned to see what was happening, but it was too late. The train could not avoid Victor, and Victor was hit by the train. Witnesses were shocked.

As Nick and the gang approached the school on their way to the tunnel, they noticed the train had stopped before entering the tunnel and witnesses were crying. Nick asked what was going on, and they learned the train had hit Victor. Nick and all the tough gangsters were in shock. Victor was new to the gang, but all the gangbangers felt sad to hear of his death. Even hard-core future criminals have emotions and feelings.

The Bonehead gang had a gang memorial service for Victor, and after that the gang began to slowly unravel. It was not a good day to be a Bonehead. They all went out to the railroad tunnel and spray-painted graffiti on the wall to honor Victor. They also left a bottle of beer near the tracks. The gangster girl-friends left flowers, and they made a white cross with the words "R.I.P. Flaco."

Some gangsters decided to leave the gang and try other things, but Nick was undecided about what he wanted to do. Stay or leave?

Nick began to drink or smoke marijuana all the time in an effort to deal with his emotions. He was depressed, but he did not want help to deal with his depression.

Chapter 17

Nick's Out-of-Control Life

Nick was unable to deal with Victor's death, and he began to use a lot of alcohol and drugs. This form of depression is not good, and using alcohol and drugs to deal with depression is dangerous as well.

Nick began to look a little frazzled. He wore the same clothing for several days in a row and stopped taking care of his personal hygiene. Nick would go days without taking a shower or even brushing his teeth.

Then Nick ran into an old friend from his old school. Ashley was back, and she was a heavy drug abuser. Ashley and her drug dealer introduced Nick to a new drug called crank, a.k.a. methamphetamine.

Nick was able to make regular contact with Ashley's meth dealer, and he slowly got hooked on meth like Ashley. Nick's physical appearance began to change, with his face breaking out in sores. His hair began to get thin, dirty, and stringy, and Nick lost a lot of weight so he was very thin and frail-looking.

As Nick roamed the area aimlessly, a second problem was drawing near. Nick was about to have his eighteenth birthday. He would no longer be considered a juvenile but an adult. Nick would not go to juvenile hall as he had so many times before; instead he was headed for adult jail and later an adult court. Nick was in the major leagues now.

That's when Nick ran into Kathy. Kathy was a kind, generous girl who loved animals and helping anyone. She was a Mother Teresa type to anyone who was in trouble. Kathy would pickup stray dogs and cats and care for them. Kathy would even help wild birds if they were injured, and her kind heart was willing to help anyone or anything that needed her.

It was late one rainy night when Kathy saw Nick walking slowly in the dark. She saw a sad look on his face as she drew near him. Kathy stopped and offered Nick a ride. Nick got into her car, and Kathy wanted to help him right away. Nick was quick to tell her only about his pain and sorrows. Kathy's tender heart was touched.

Nick did not have to go home because he was an adult, and he did not want to argue with his mother about being high again. Nick was in a lot of denial.

Nick asked Kathy to drop him off at his drug dealer's house. Kathy did not know the neighborhood, and it was good she did not stay.

But Kathy was still bothered by Nick's sad story, and she desperately wanted to help him. A couple of days later, Kathy again saw Nick walking down the street. She stopped to offer him a ride. Nick was high again, and he did not remember speaking with Kathy that rainy night or the ride she'd given him.

Nick wanted to break into a house so he could steal another person's property to get his next high. Nick told Kathy to wait for him in front of the house until he was able to collect a few things. Kathy did not know the house Nick was entering was not his own.

About ten minutes later, Nick asked Kathy to drop him off at his drug dealer's house. Kathy was very naive, and she followed Nick inside the dealer's house. Nick was right at home, but Kathy did not understand what was about to happen to her.

The drug dealer needed a ride to pick up more drugs, and he offered Nick a free drug sample if Kathy would drive them over to the drug pick-up area. Kathy offered to take them in her car, not knowing what Nick and the dealer were picking up.

Kathy was very trusting, and Nick and his dealer took advantage of her kind heart. Nick and the drug dealer went inside the drug house to make the drug deal as Kathy waited outside in her car. As Nick and the drug dealer entered the house they decided to steal the drugs instead of buying them. Of course, this was not well received by the drug dealer in the drug house and he grabbed a gun and shot at Nick and his drug dealer as they ran from the house unharmed. Kathy heard the shots and froze with fear. As Nick and the drug dealer entered the car, they yelled at Kathy to drive—"Go, go!"

Kathy wanted to know what had happened, and why did she have to drive so fast? Was everyone at the house okay? What was going on? Kathy did not ask enough questions, because Nick and the drug dealer could have been homicide suspects. What happened inside the house? If Kathy heard gunshots, someone could be hurt; and now she was involved because she drove the getaway car.

Nick told Kathy she heard firecrackers and that everything was fine. Kathy bought their lies—Nick was good at lying.

Kathy drove back to the drug dealer's house, and Nick wanted her to leave for now. Nick wanted Kathy to return in a couple of hours to pick him up again. Nick wanted to get high with his dealer.

Naive Kathy did return, and Nick was indeed high. Kathy decided to take Nick to her house so she could feed Nick and try to help him. But Nick was now beyond help. He needed professional help.

Kathy invited her girlfriends from school over to her house so they could meet Nick. Kathy's friends were not impressed with Nick, and they saw right away that he was trouble. They tried to warn Kathy about Nick, but she thought she could help him.

They left Kathy alone with Nick, and then it happened. Nick wanted to borrow Kathy's car. Kathy said no because Nick was high. Nick suddenly turned violent, and he attacked her. He forced her into her car and drove her to a drug house. Kathy tried to reason with Nick, but he refused to listen. Nick took Kathy by force and against her will.

When Kathy's parents arrived home, they found their house in disarray. They called Kathy's friends and learned she had invited Nick to their house. Kathy's parents did not know a Nick. Who was Nick?

When the first police officer arrived, he learned Kathy had taken her cellphone, and they were able to track the cellphone through GPS. The dispatcher contacted the cellphone carrier, and they pinged the cellphone to get a current location. The cellphone was at a well-known drug dealer's house.

Police officers converged on the drug dealer's house looking for Kathy. The cellphone was there, but not Kathy. Kathy was with Nick, and Nick was driving Kathy's car. A BOLF (be on the lookout for) was issued for Kathy's car.

Since I was very familiar with Nick, I drove to all of Nick's hangouts searching for Kathy or her car. Every police officer was searching for Kathy. The BOLF was statewide, and there was nowhere Nick could hide.

Then I just happened to see Nick in Kathy's car. Nick spotted me, and the car chase was on. I drove after Nick, and he refused to stop and pull over. I did not want to hurt either Kathy or Nick.

The car chase went on for miles, with other police cars joining in. Nick was driving wildly and recklessly. The decision was made to end the chase when the police helicopter had the car in sight. The idea was to stop chasing Nick and let the police helicopter follow the car until it stopped. All police officers would follow the car's direction on the police car radios. Once Nick saw the police cars had stopped chasing him, he would slow down and eventually stop.

The plan worked because Nick did stop after driving to his mother's house. Nick and Kathy were surrounded by police officers, and Nick gave up without resistance. Kathy was doing well, and she was sent to a hospital for a physical.

Nick was transported to the police station, and as usual he refused to say anything about what had occurred with Kathy. Nick was booked into adult jail and a bail hearing was set for the next day. Nick was appointed a public defender, and his bail was set at half a million dollars. Nick was unable to make bail. It was not looking good for him.

Kathy was interviewed, and she agreed to testify against Nick in open court. Nick's public defender was able to make a deal, and Nick was offered five to fifteen years in prison if he pled guilty. Nick decided to take the deal.

Chapter 18

The Good-Bye

The last time I saw Nick was the day he was placed on a prison bus. Nick left a message at the police station for me to visit him at the jail. He wanted to say a personal good-bye.

The prison bus was headed for San Quentin State Prison. Nick was now in the big leagues—state prison. I went to say good-bye and good luck to a kid I'd known since elementary school. A kid I'd known through good times and bad times.

Nick was placed in protective custody because he was a gang member. Everywhere he went, he was kept separate from the mainstream inmates. The mainstream inmates wanted to kill Nick because his gang had caused a lot of problems in their neighborhood. Gang members don't call the police if there is a problem because they would rather handle the problems themselves. The police take a report and too much time to take care of business. Nick had a reputation for causing many problems.

Nick was all chained up as he approached me to say his good-bye. Nick was wearing his blue CDC (California Department of Corrections) jumpsuit, waist chains, and leg shackles. It was sad to see Nick walking down the long jail hall.

When he drew close to me, Nick smiled and said, "I should have listened to you, OG. You were right all the time; I should have listened."

I extended my hand to shake Nick's. I said, "I wish you luck, Nick, and I'll check with your mother every now and then; so keep in contact with her."

Nick choked back his tears, and he continued to walk down the hall to the waiting prison bus. The bus was loaded with future inmates, and Nick was now a new inmate.

I watched the prison bus back up from the loading port and slowly leave the county jail for state prison. California has more than twenty-five prisons, and the prison system is full to the max with inmates. To outsiders Nick is now just a prison number, but I can still see little Nick as an innocent kid who mixed with the wrong crowd and admired the wrong role models.

What a sad ending for what could have been a good ending! Good luck, Nick, wherever you are.

ABOOKS

ALIVE Book Publishing and ALIVE Publishing Group
are imprints of Advanced Publishing LLC,
3200 A Danville Blvd., Suite 204, Alamo, California 94507

Telephone: 925.837.7303 Fax: 925.837.6951
www.alivebookpublishing.com